HAMELIN

Just for Alex and George

1 2 3 4 5 6 7 8 9 10

Library of Congress Cataloging in Publication Data:

Ross, Tony.
   The Pied Piper of Hamelin.

   SUMMARY: The Pied Piper pipes the village free of
rats and when the villagers refuse to pay him for the
service, he pipes away their children, too.
   1. Pied Piper of Hamelin—Legends. 2. Legends—
Germany—Hameln. 3. Hameln—History—Juvenile literature.
[1. Pied Piper of Hamelin. 2. Folklore—
Germany. 3. Hameln—History—Fiction] I. Piper of
Hamelin. II. Title.
PZ8.1.R693Pi 1978 823'.9'14 [398.2] [E] 77-24056
ISBN 0-688-41824-4

ISBN 0-688-51824-9 lib. bdg.

Printed in Great Britain by
T. & A. Constable Ltd., Edinburgh

the Pied Piper of Hamelin

retold and illustrated by Tony Ross

Lothrop, Lee & Shepard, New York

Lothrop, Lee & Shepard Company. A Division of William Morrow & Co., Inc. New York
Published in the United States in 1978. Copyright © 1977 by Tony Ross
First published in Great Britain in 1977 by Andersen Press Ltd.

Long, long ago, when towns were very small, the people of
Hamelin lived in fear and misery.
The town itself was pretty enough, with lots of
cakeshops, and parks to play in. Yet the people crept
about the streets, peering this way and that, jumping at
the slightest sound.
The reason for this unhappy state of affairs was . . .

RATS! Millions of rats lived in Hamelin. They were large, fat rats, with big teeth and nasty tempers. Nobody knew *why* there were so many rats; perhaps it was because Hamelin was such a nice place to live that all the rats in Germany moved there. They prowled the streets in gangs, squeaking, and generally making nuisances of themselves.

They chased the cats and the dogs.

They jumped out of holes in the walls and danced up and down on the furniture.
They nested in people's best clothes.

They even ate the cakes in the shop windows.

The Mayor and the Town Council tried all ways to rid Hamelin of the rats.
They met every Tuesday to argue over new ideas. They invented all sorts of traps.
They even built a clockwork cat . . .

. . . with big iron teeth, and fast wheels, but nothing ever worked.

The Mayor didn't know *what* to do about the rats, but the people of Hamelin expected him to do *something*!

One day, the Mayor and the Council were holding a
meeting on the table. They often met on the table
because of the rats on the floor. Suddenly they noticed a
stranger standing by the door. His clothes were
half red and half yellow.
A flute was tucked into his belt.
He spoke politely, in a soft voice.
"Sirs, I have heard tell of
your rats, and for a
thousand gold pieces
I can rid your town
of them."
"Yes, yes!" cried
the Mayor and
Council together,
wobbling on
the table.

Putting his pipe to his lips, the Piper
started to play a thin, magical tune.
The rats stopped teasing the Town Council
and looked around, blissful smiles on their
nasty faces. The Piper turned and stepped
into the street, the rats skipping along
behind him to the tune of the pipe.
Through the streets he strode, followed by a
horde of rats that danced out of every nook
and cranny.

The Mayor and Council watched in amazement as the
Pied Piper disappeared through the town gate with his
squealing, leaping company.
The mad procession took the road towards the River
Weser. On reaching the water's edge, the Piper crouched
on a boulder. His music quickened as the rats streamed
past, slipping and sliding on the river bank.

In their hundreds the rats danced into the river, to be swirled away in the fast waters.

However, one rat, who was a little deaf and could hear only snatches of the Piper's tune, kept his wits about him. He managed to scramble to safety on a rock.

The rat who escaped didn't return to the town. Instead, he took to the road, and warned every rat he met of the terrible things that happened to rats in Hamelin.

His work done, the Pied Piper returned to Hamelin to claim his thousand pieces of gold.

But the Mayor was not an honest man. Seeing that all the rats had gone, he saw no reason to pay the Piper.

Angered at being cheated, the Piper pointed a quivering finger at the Mayor.

"This is one promise you will regret breaking!" he snapped.

Putting his pipe to his lips, the Piper turned on his heel and stormed back into the street.

Once more the Pied Piper strode through Hamelin, playing a wild tune, his cloak streaming out behind him. The Mayor watched in horror, unable to move, as children began to follow the music. They stopped their games, they climbed out of their windows, drawn by the sound of the enchanted pipe.

The Piper headed for the river, but at the last minute
swung away to the west.
Night was falling when he halted the children at a
mountain. At an unheard command, a huge door opened
in the mountainside and, laughing and dancing, the
children disappeared inside.
The door closed as mysteriously as it had opened. The
Piper tucked his pipe into his belt and melted into the
silence.

Not all of Hamelin's children were locked inside the mountain. One little boy, Jan, had hurt his leg and he couldn't dance as fast as the rest. Unnoticed, Jan had followed on behind. It was dark when he reached the mountain; he had followed the footprints in the dust, and the faint sounds of the music.

In the moonlight, he stood and stared at the bare hillside, where the tracks ended. Then sadly, and all alone, Jan turned and limped back to Hamelin.

Poor Jan was the only child left in Hamelin.

As he had no one to play with, all the grown-ups made a great fuss over him. They listened again and again to his story of how the children had vanished into the mountain.

From that day on, the townspeople waited in vain for their children to return.

And the Mayor? Well, he lived to rue the day he had tried to cheat the Pied Piper of Hamelin.

But, what of the children?
When the mountain shut out the music of the magic
pipe, the spell was broken and the children became
frightened. Stumbling about in the dark, they found a
steep passage. One little boy called Klaus, braver than
the rest, set off down the passage. Hand in hand, the
others followed the sound of his footsteps. At last, the
children poured out of the far side of the mountain into
a lost and beautiful valley. There were clear streams,
lots of peach trees and exotic birds.

There were *no* roads, *no* grown-ups, and *no* rats!
Over the years, as the children grew up, they built a
beautiful city. Klaus was made a Duke and looked
after everybody.

Even today, the descendants of the children of Hamelin
live happily in their secret land. They play all day,
they eat peaches and sausages, and sing happy songs.
I know . . . I've been there.